Her revealing dress

Duffy

QUARTET BOOKS
LONDON NEW YORK

Dedicated to
Angela, Simon, Rachel,
Geraldine, Anne-Marie, Micheal,
Mary, Minnie, Toby, Oscar,
Wooly and Nigel

First published by Quartet Books Limited 1986
A member of the Namara Group
27/29 Goodge Street, London W1P 1FD

Duffy
Her revealing dress.
1. Women—Great Britain—Social conditions—Pictorial works
I. Title
305.4′2′0941 HQ1593

ISBN 0 7043 0029 X

Printed and bound in Great Britain by
Hazell Watson & Viney Limited,
Member of the BPCC Group,
Aylesbury, Bucks

Duffy was born in Liverpool and still lives there. He entered art school at the age of thirteen and this led to several years in London as a lithographer and designer. During the 1970s he developed his visual vocabulary through performance and the media. Since this period at art college, he has combined a successful commitment to fine-art teaching with more entrepreneurial work, establishing the Arena Art Studios and becoming a founder member and Chairman of the British Art and Design Association. He has had a succession of exhibitions throughout the UK and in West Germany, with important one-man shows in London and New York. The British and American press and visual media have reviewed his work with enthusiasm which has led to some major awards. The common threads that run through all his art are the observation of and comment on human behaviour, human relationships and the trials and tribulations of the individual making his or her way through life's maze.

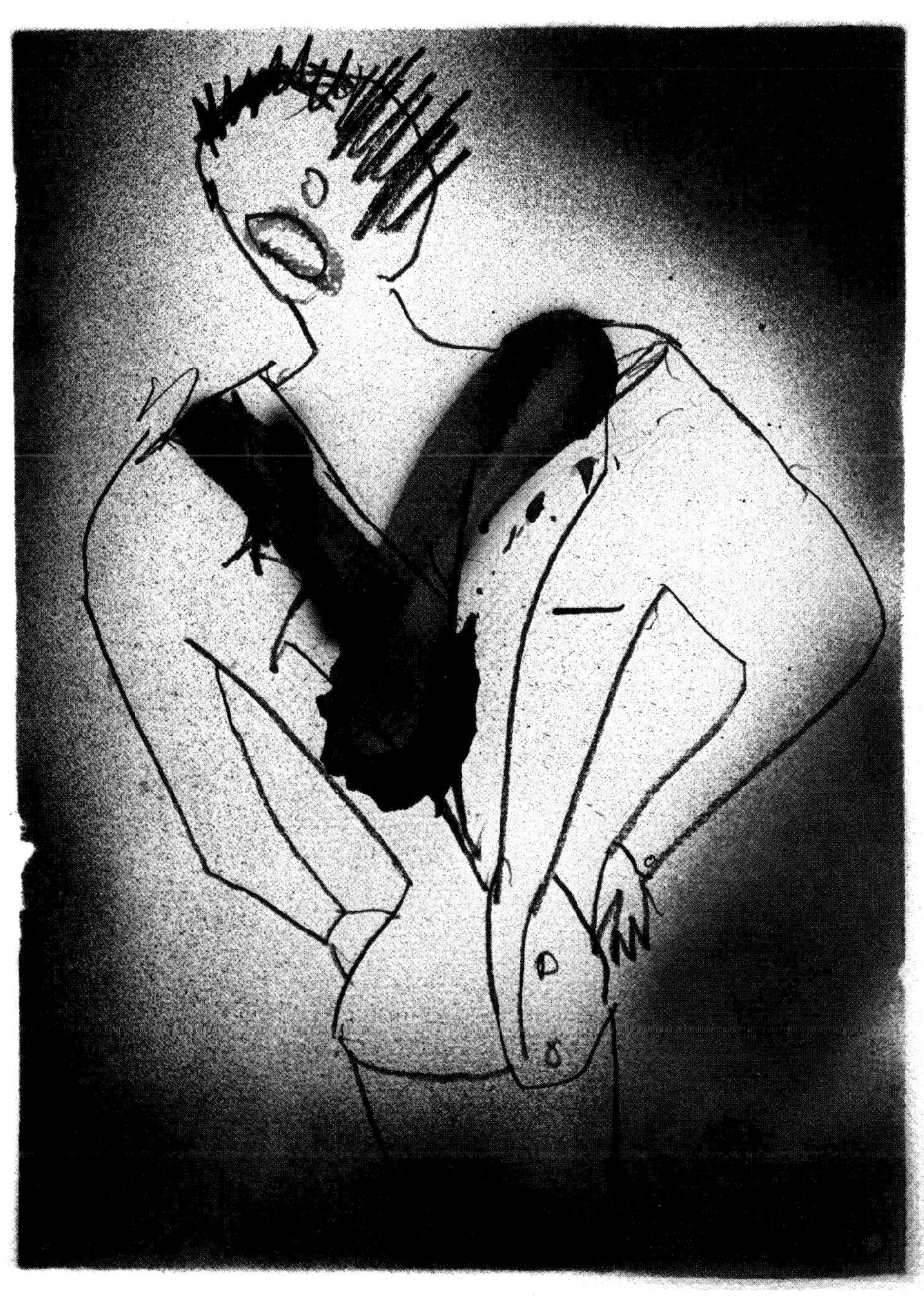

She extended her mouth
and tested the full authority
of her new lipstick

*Men would stare
at her revealing dress.*

She ~~They~~ manipulated the emotion
that the space between them created.

The dress helped her body to speak
she wandered if she could control
what it was saying

He admired her presence
and looked forward to her company.

She supplied the image
and he supplied the money.

Her walk said everything.

During the night.

ON HER WAY HOME
SHE THOUGHT OF PAUL.

APPLYING MAKE-UP
SHE THOUGHT OF HIM MORE.

ON HER WAY OUT
SHE WAVED A TAXI.

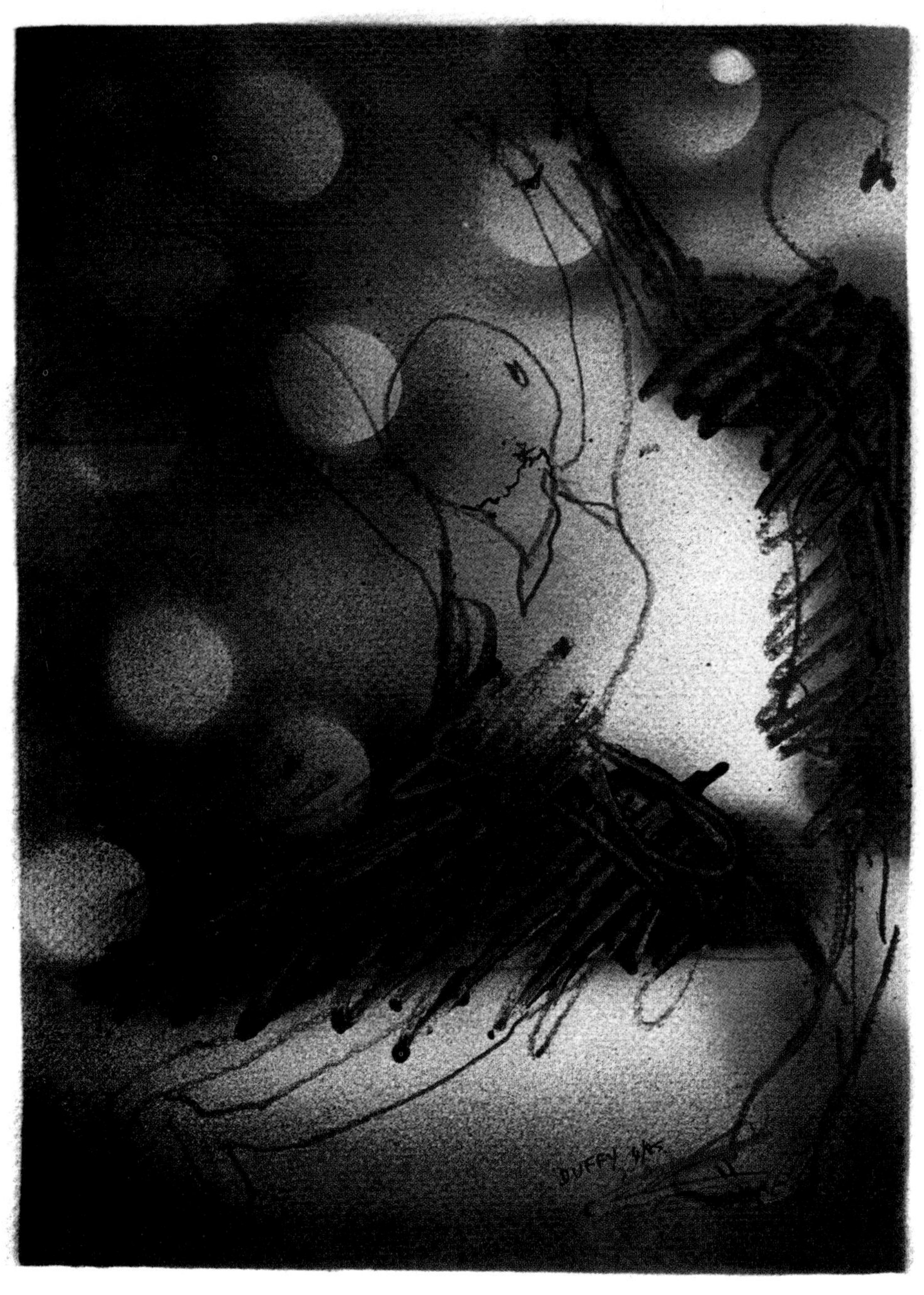

DURING THE DANCE
SHE LEFT THE FLOOR.

DURING THE NIGHT
SHE THOUGHT ^ OF GEORGE.
ONLY

Practice makes perfect.

As the rain fell
so did her image.

*She knew he was her only
sincere audience, but never told him.*

She swayed her hips,
flashed a smile and danced.
Practice makes perfect.

Sex with ~~his wife~~ her was like approaching traffic lights on green, you never knew if they would change rapidly.

Below the 'make-up'
her face pleaded for recognition.

She preferred plain men,
they were more grateful.

She applied make-up like an expert plasterer
½" ~~thick~~ thick with a very smooth finish.

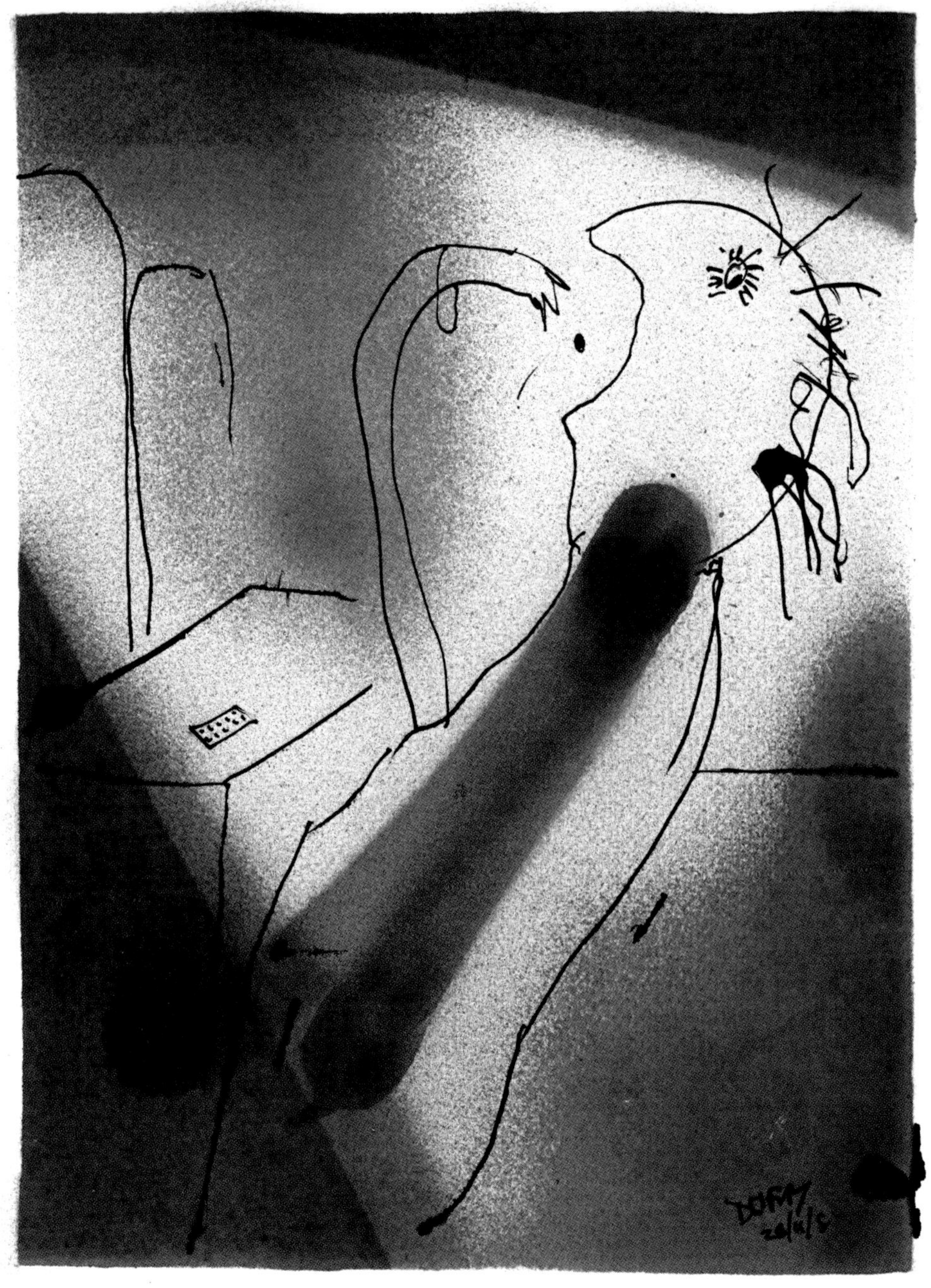

TAKE 1. She took the pill
and wished for a man.

TAKE. 2. She took the pill
it was all part of the image

After the leg wax she felt fresh,
smooth and extremely attractive.
Men continued not to notice her.

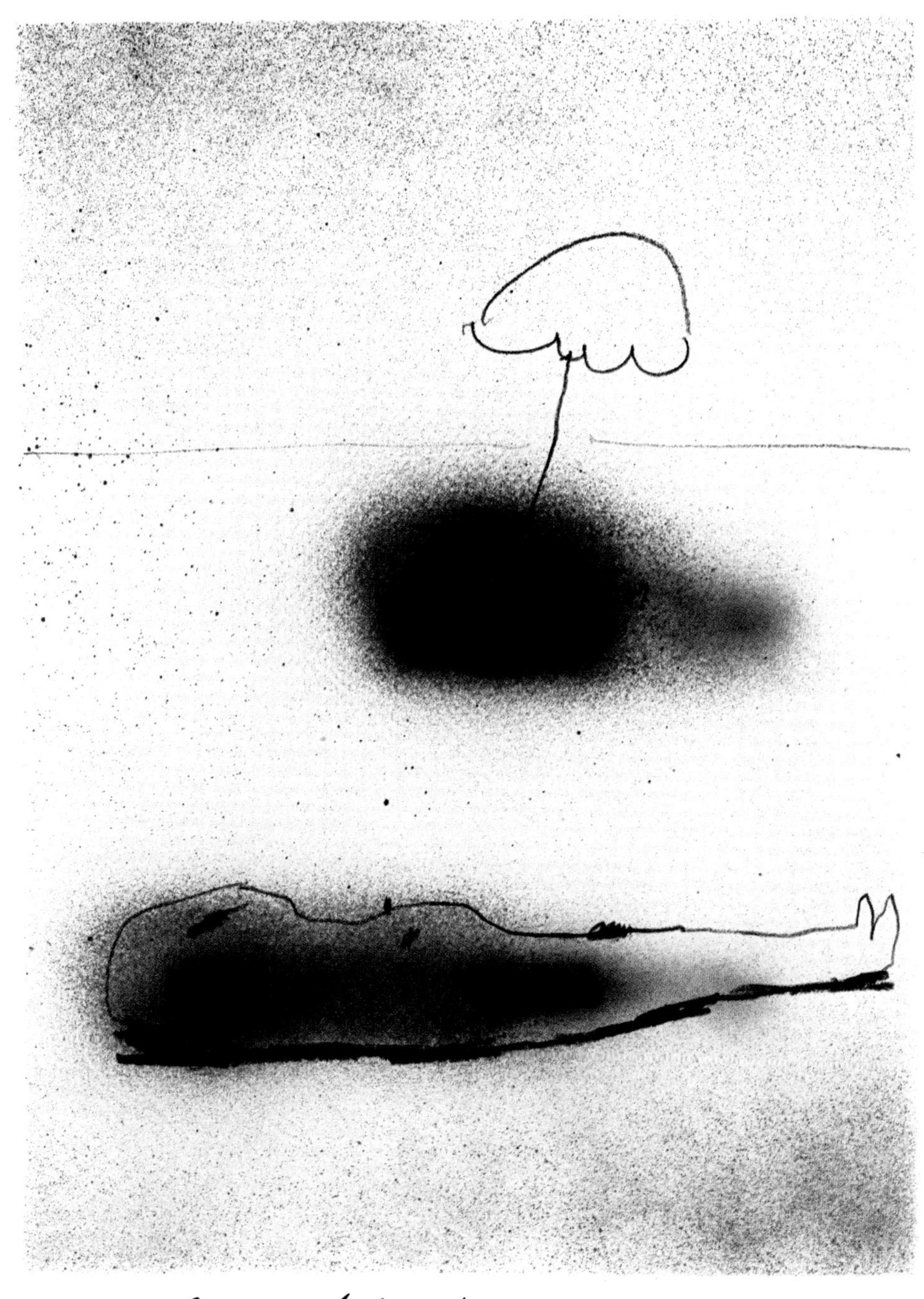

As she cooked in the sun
she thought of minority groups,
and the plight of the starving
in Africa.

She screamed in silence
and washed another plate

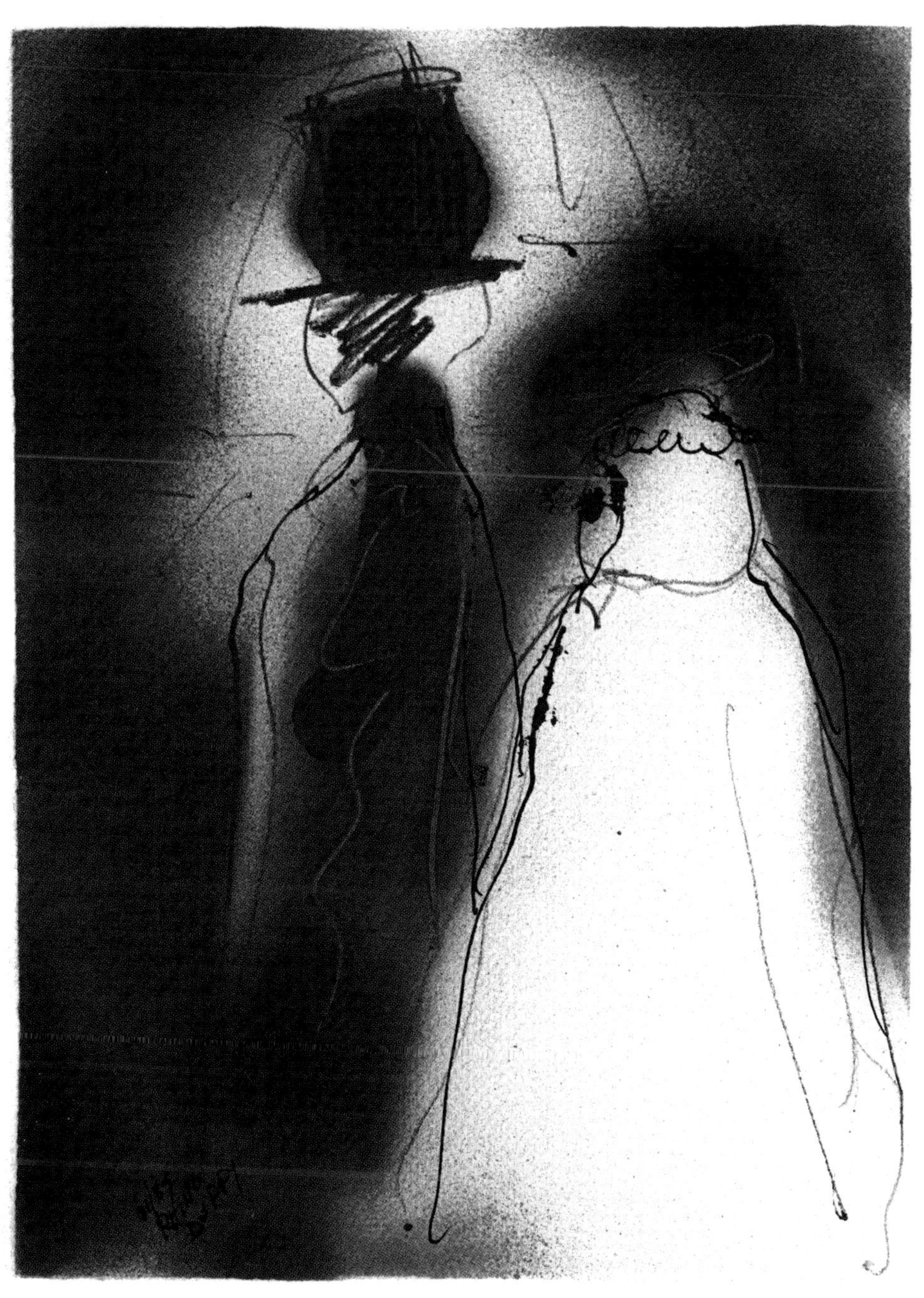

Eventhough he was a manual worker
she would always remember him
in top hat and tails.

Marriage was a reality
that stayed an illusion

They cut the cake
and smiled for the camera

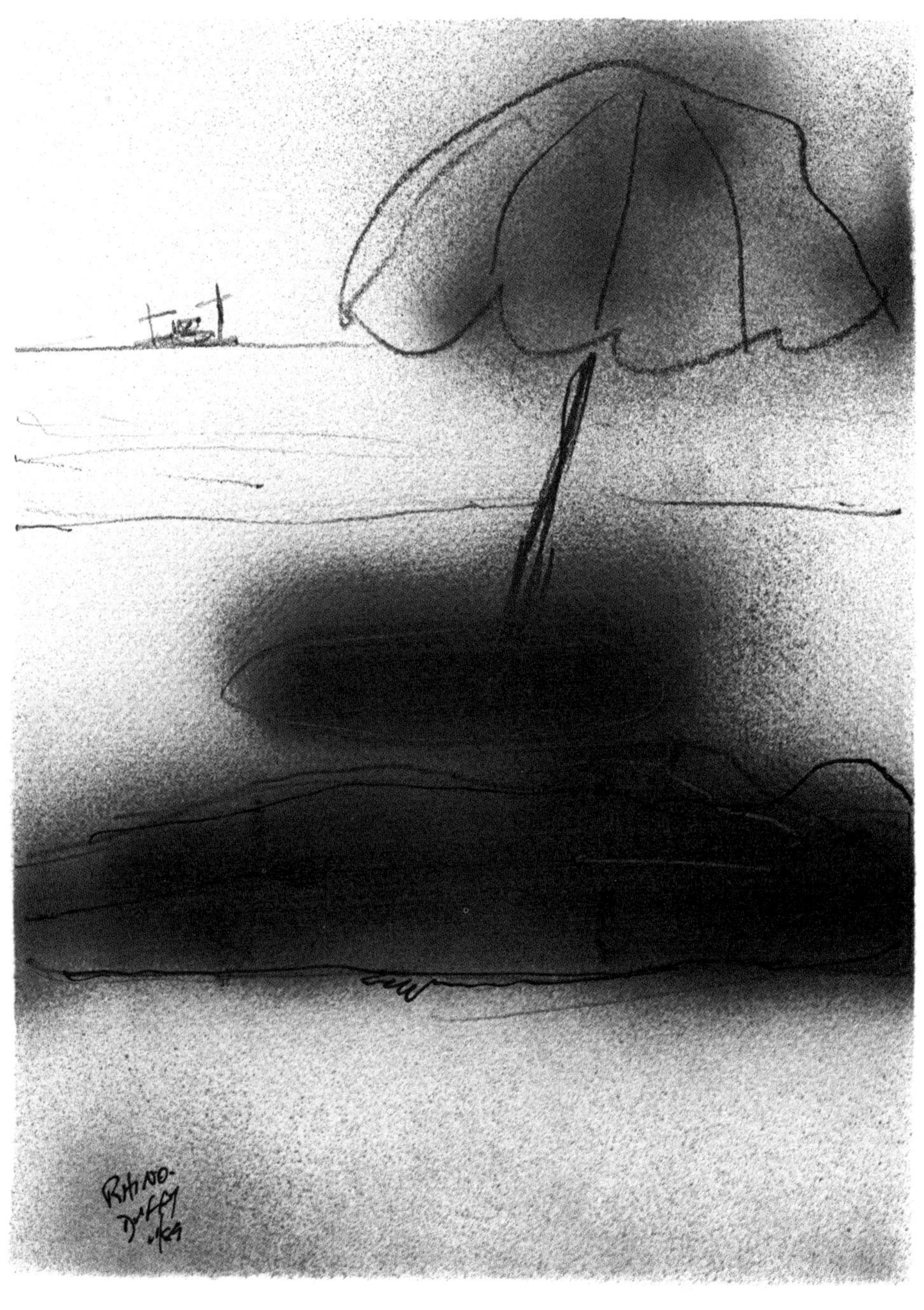

Like a beached whale
she lay motionless,
in a layer of oil.

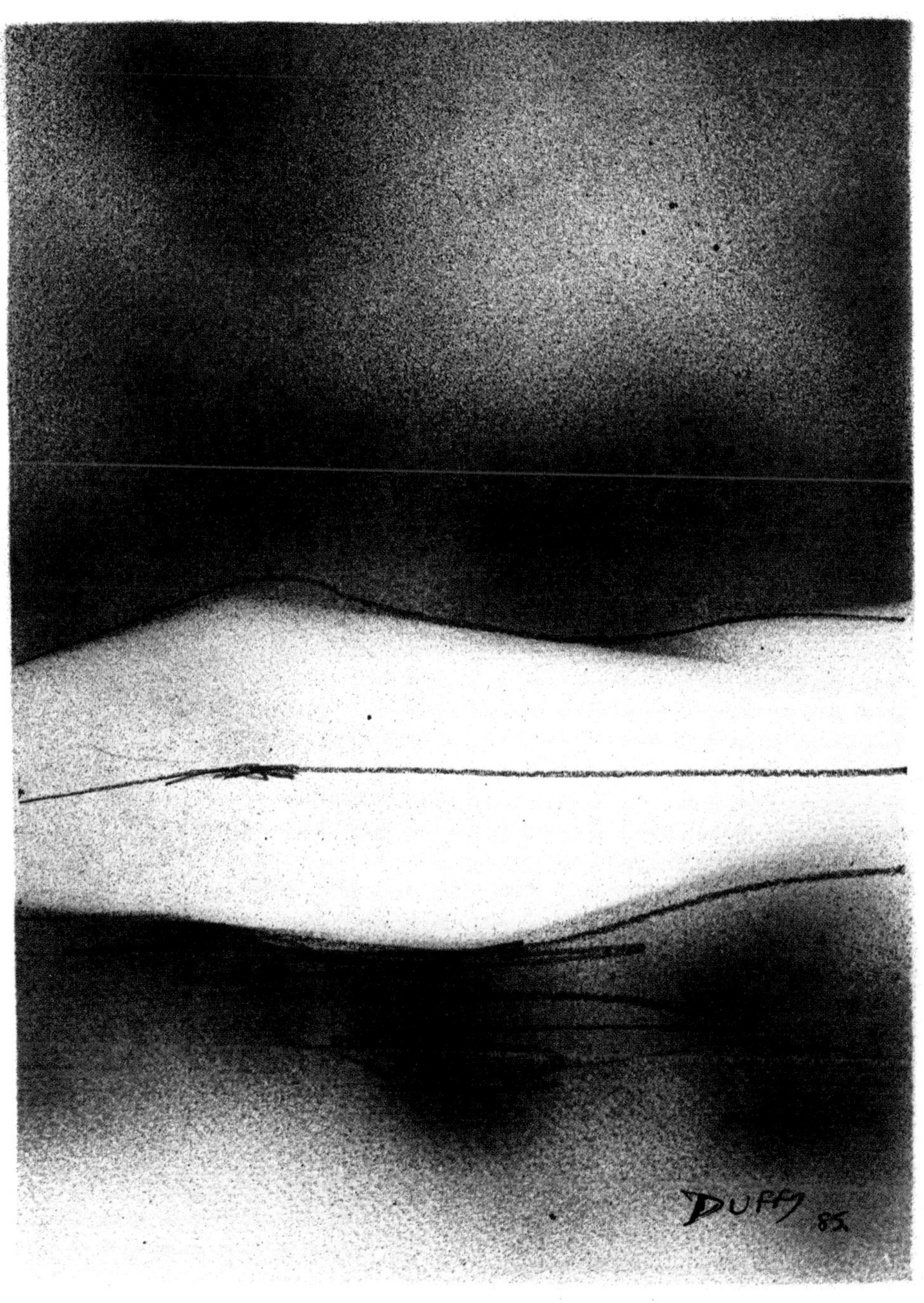

They ~~the~~ had see the way he drove his car fast, clean and efficient. She ~~had~~ didn't know any better, she'd only had one driver.

It takes Two
to make Three!

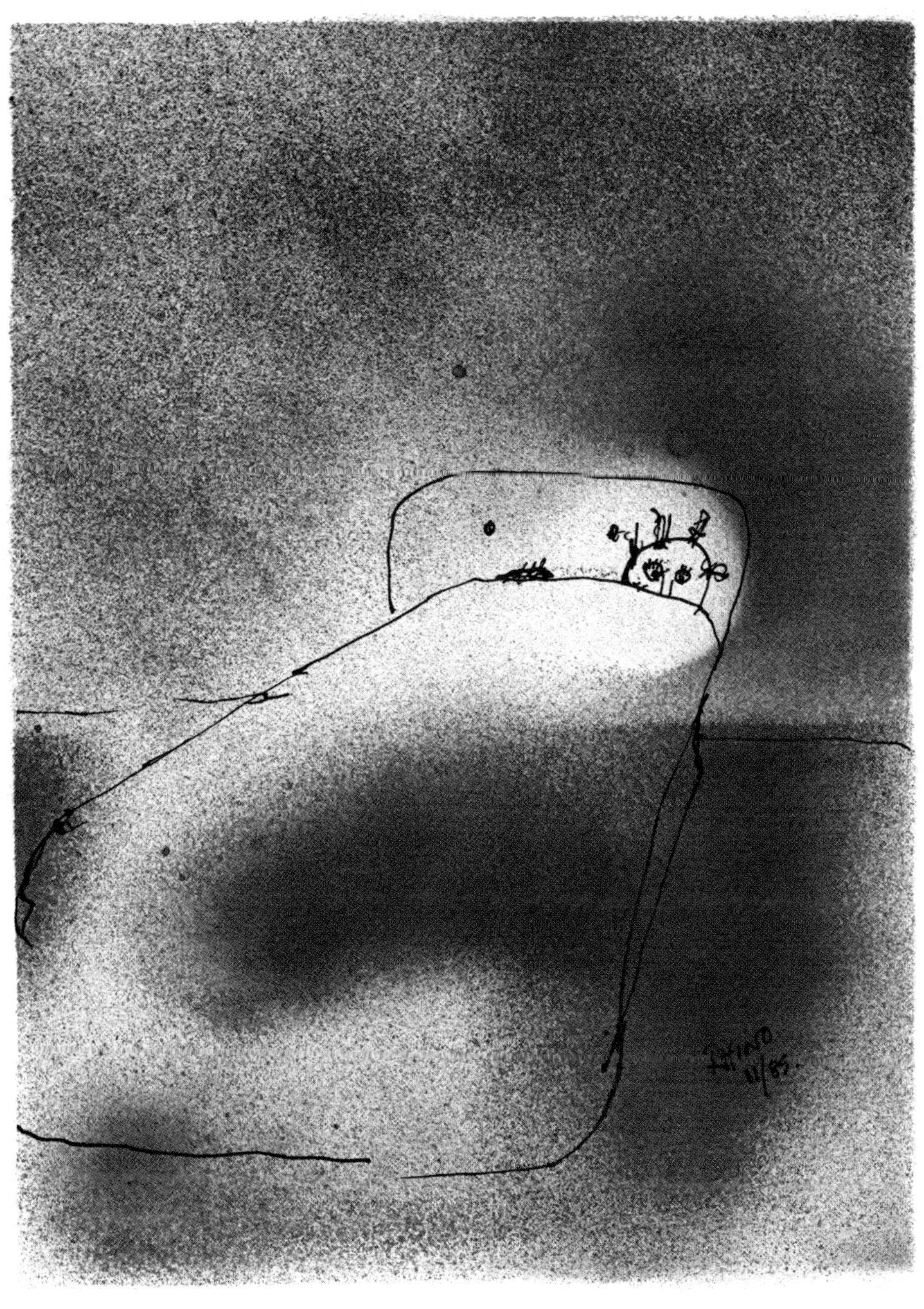

TAKE. 1. After, she lay there silently,
and wondered what a girl should do next.

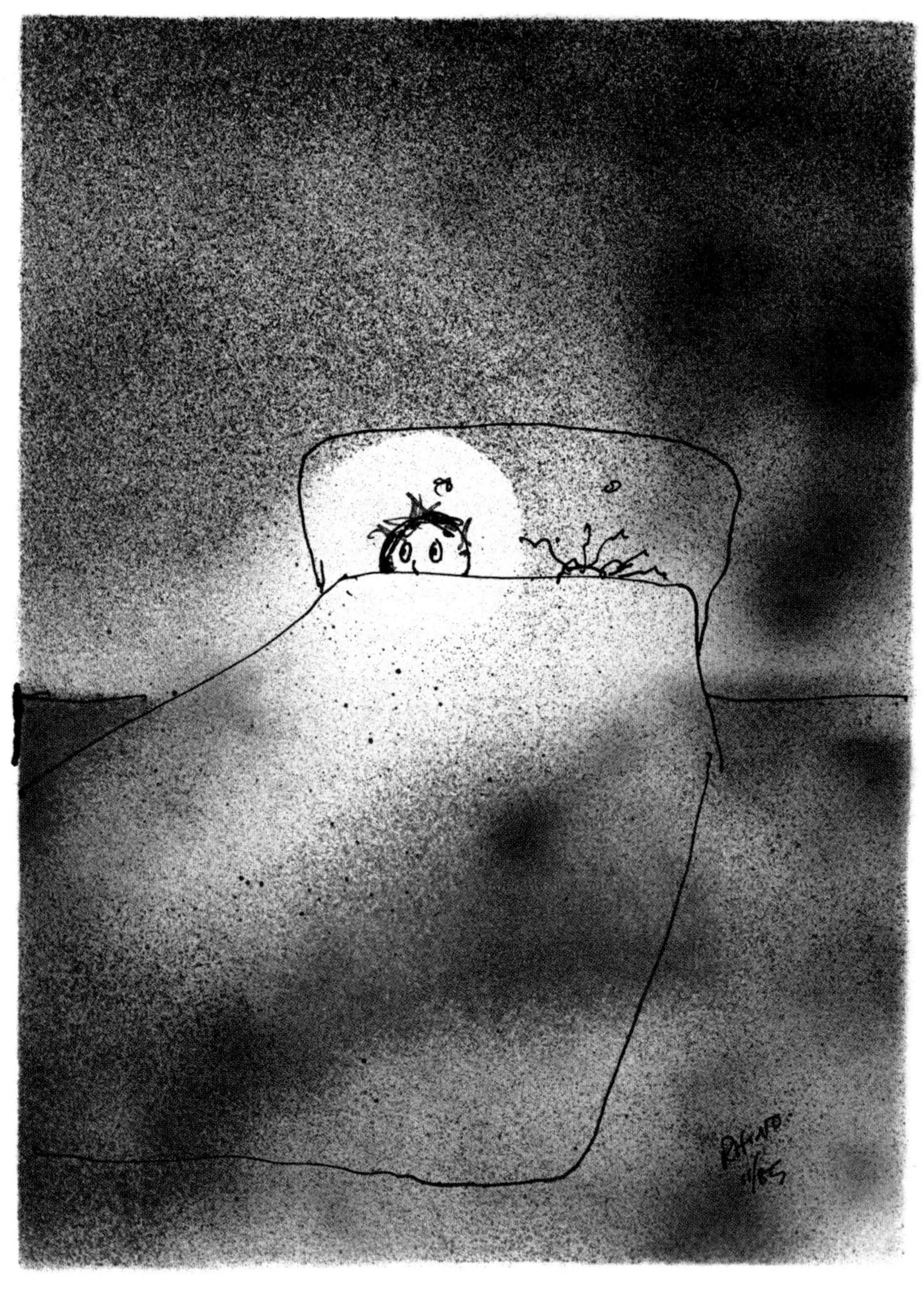

TAKE.2. After, she lay silently.
He wandered what he was supposed to do next.

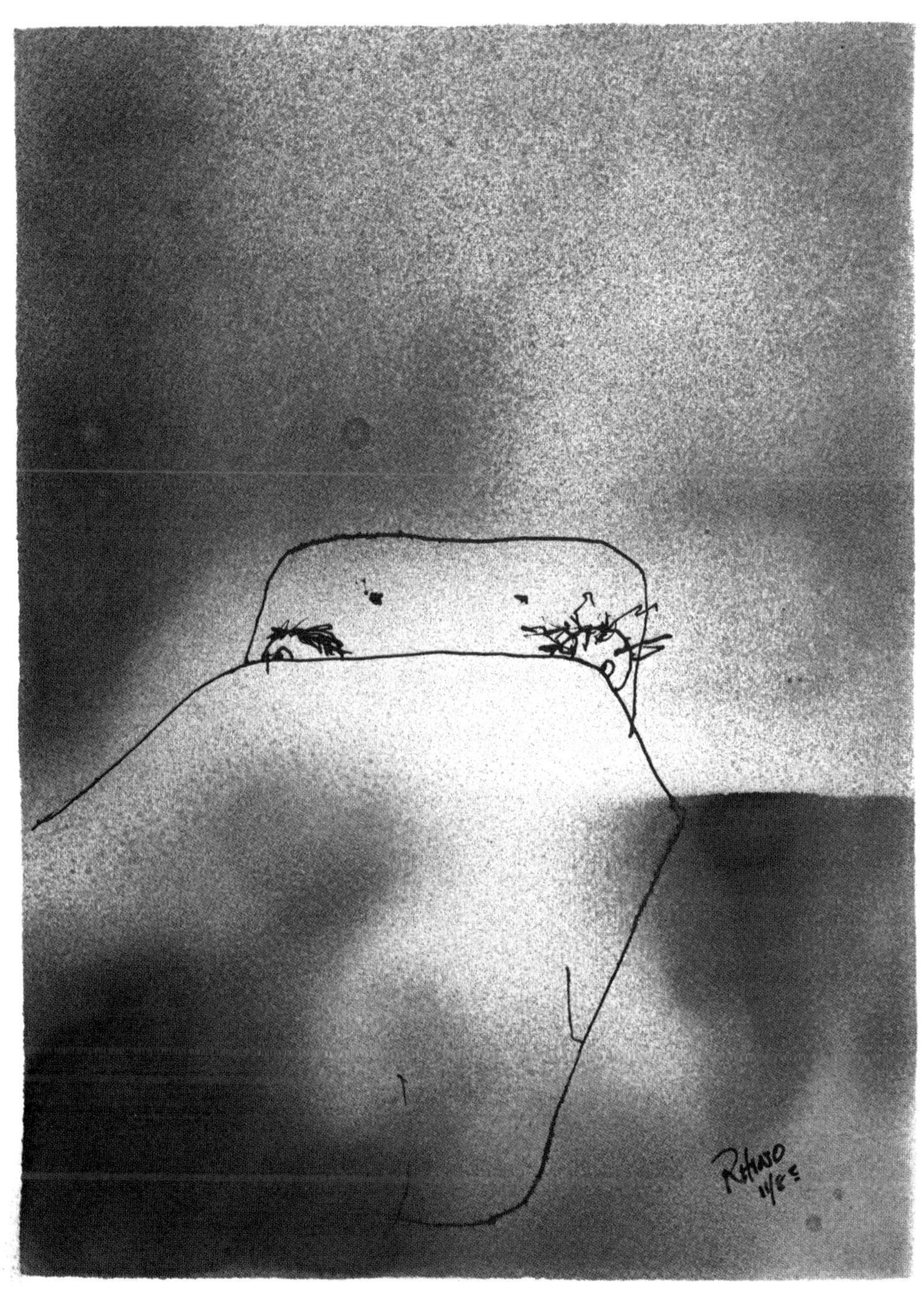

TAKE 3. After, they layed there silently wandering if that was it.

Feeling Important.

*She was the boss's secretary
but would smile at
visitors!*

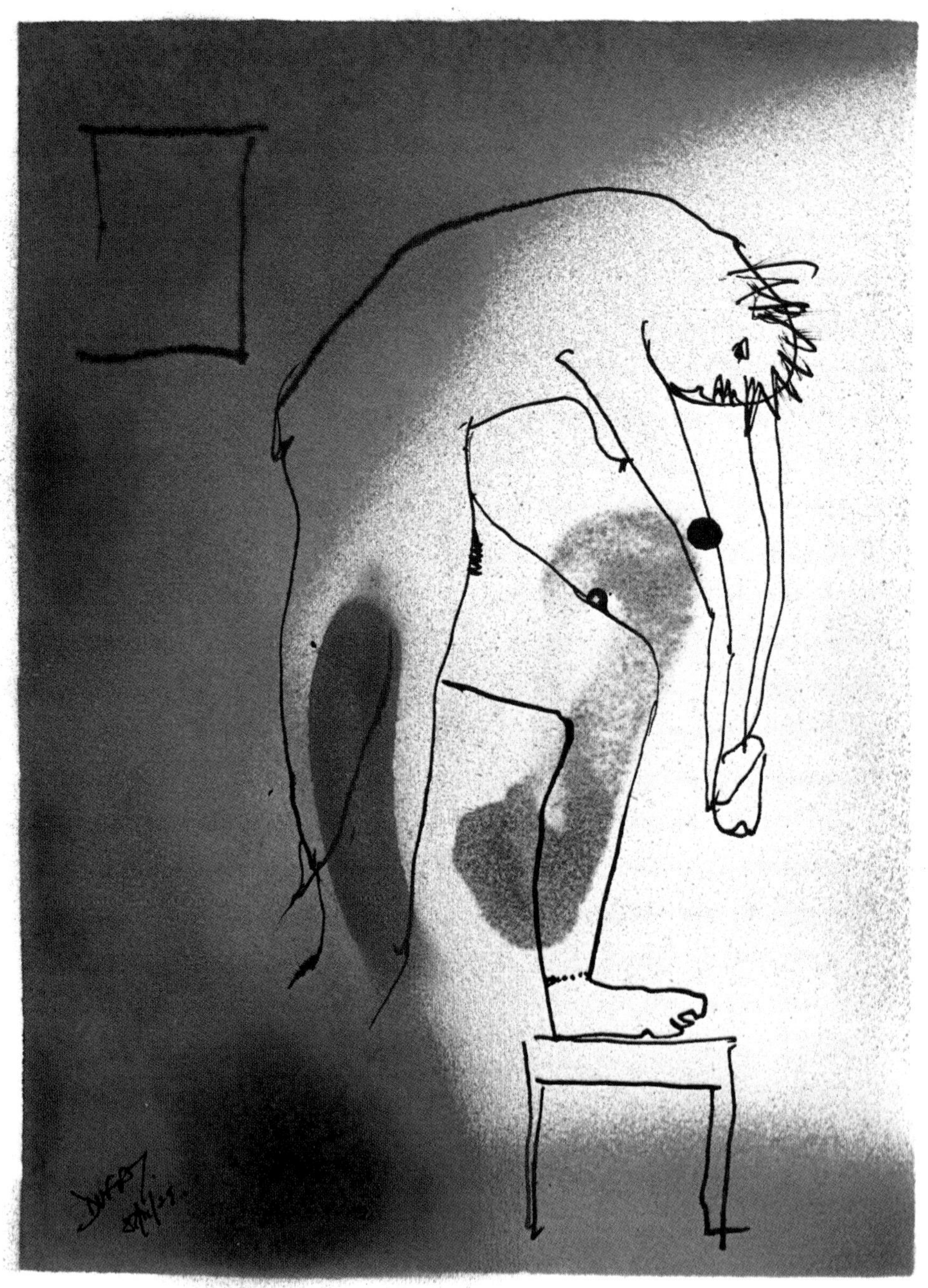

Whilst bending over to gently slide into her see through panties, she admired the feminine delicacy of the fine chain about her ankles.

She hovered in the shop light
and felt important

Her reflection danced
with shop mannequins.
She ignored it.

The morning kiss was a moments cavity

He didn't know what "erogenous zone" meant, but she did!

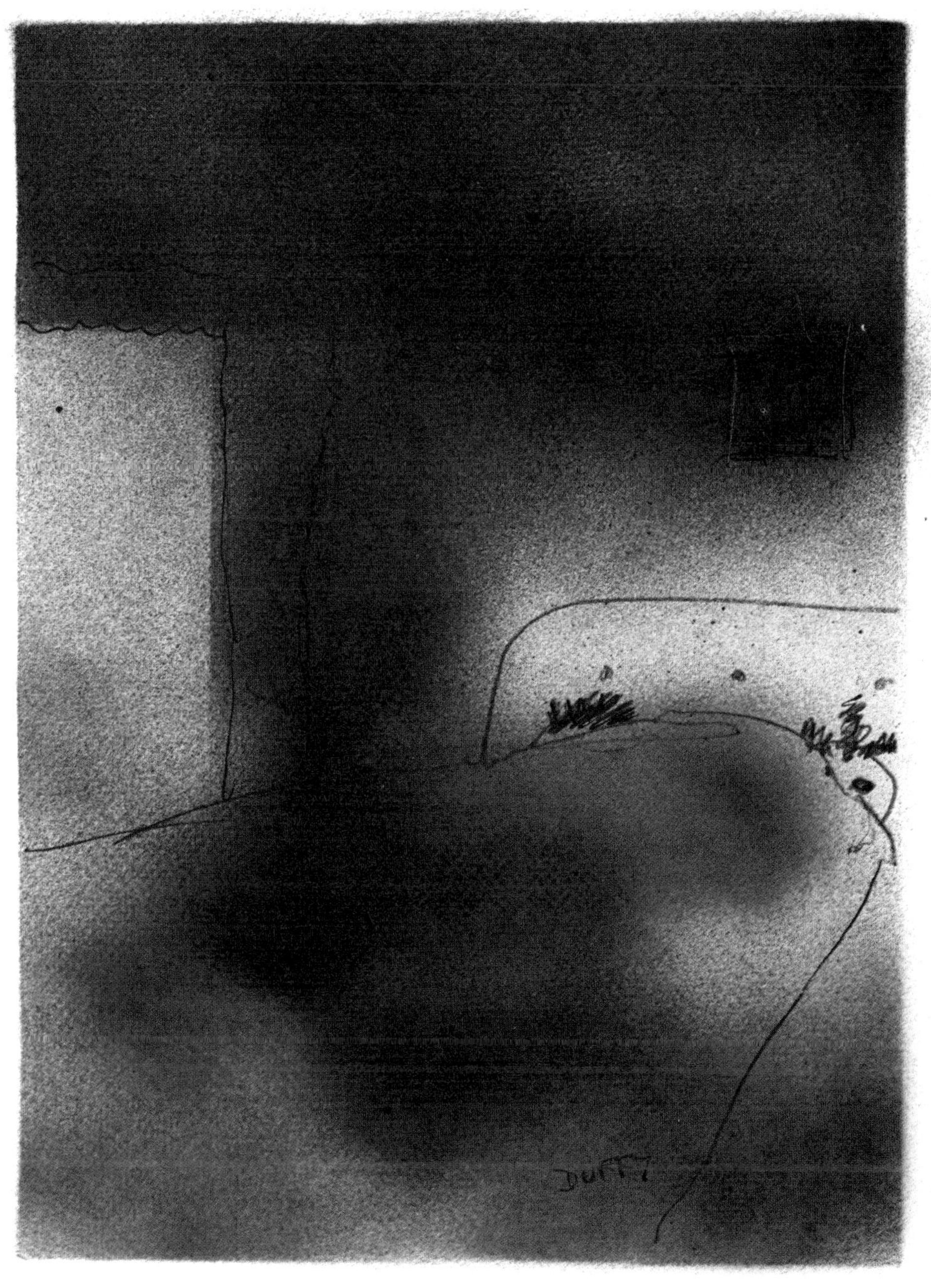

As his hand moved across her thigh she thought of body language and the simplicity of traffic lights. With the slightest movement she could signal stop, go or even keep him waiting.

Always happy??

In the morning traffic
she would apply her make-up.

At the office desk
she was ~~very~~ always happy.

Alone with friends
she sat on the floor.

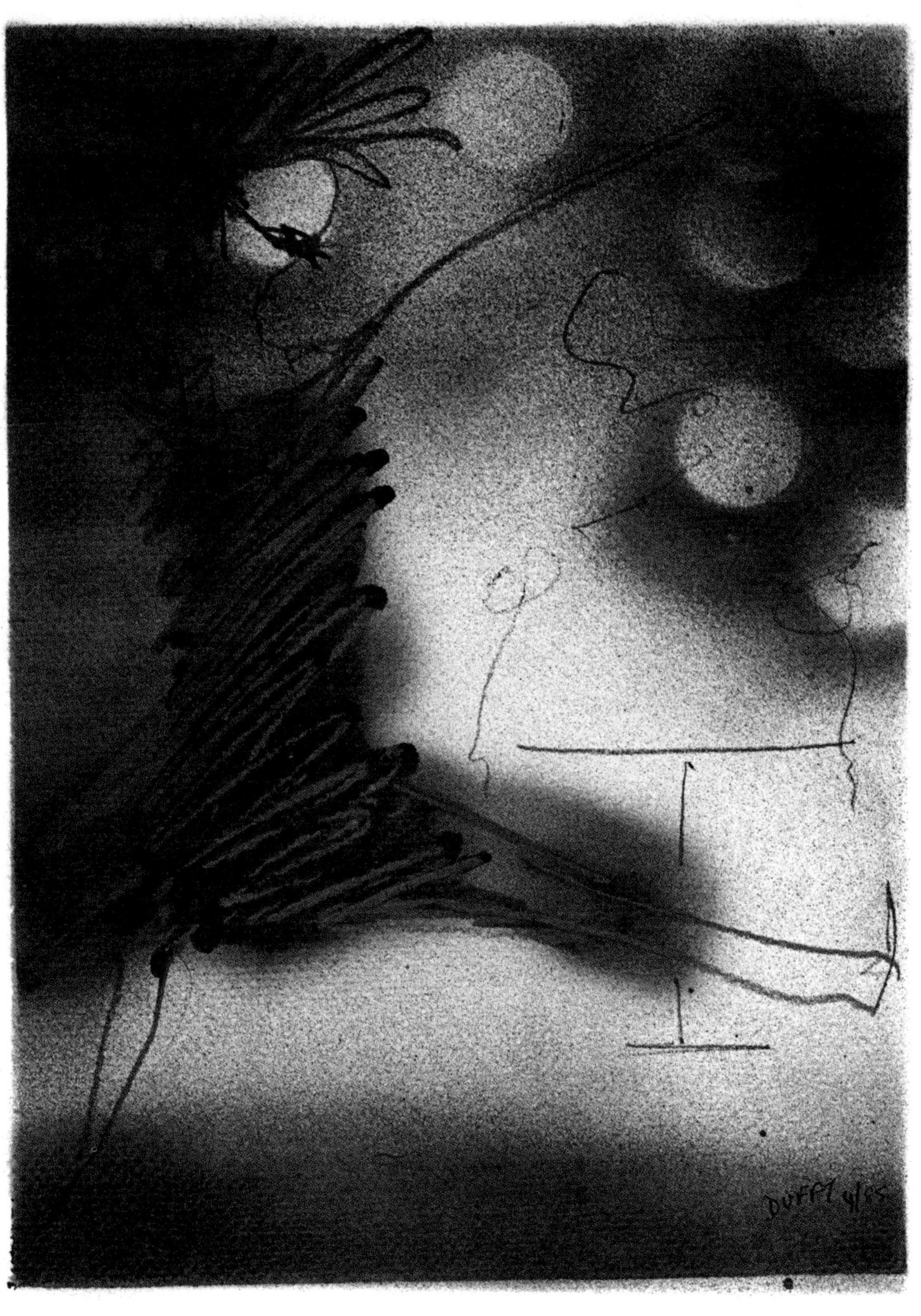

In the evening life
she fooled them all.

At home, she hated the front door.

Natalie Poirel

She hated weak men,
especially him

Hairy legs are masculine
she had to be feminine.

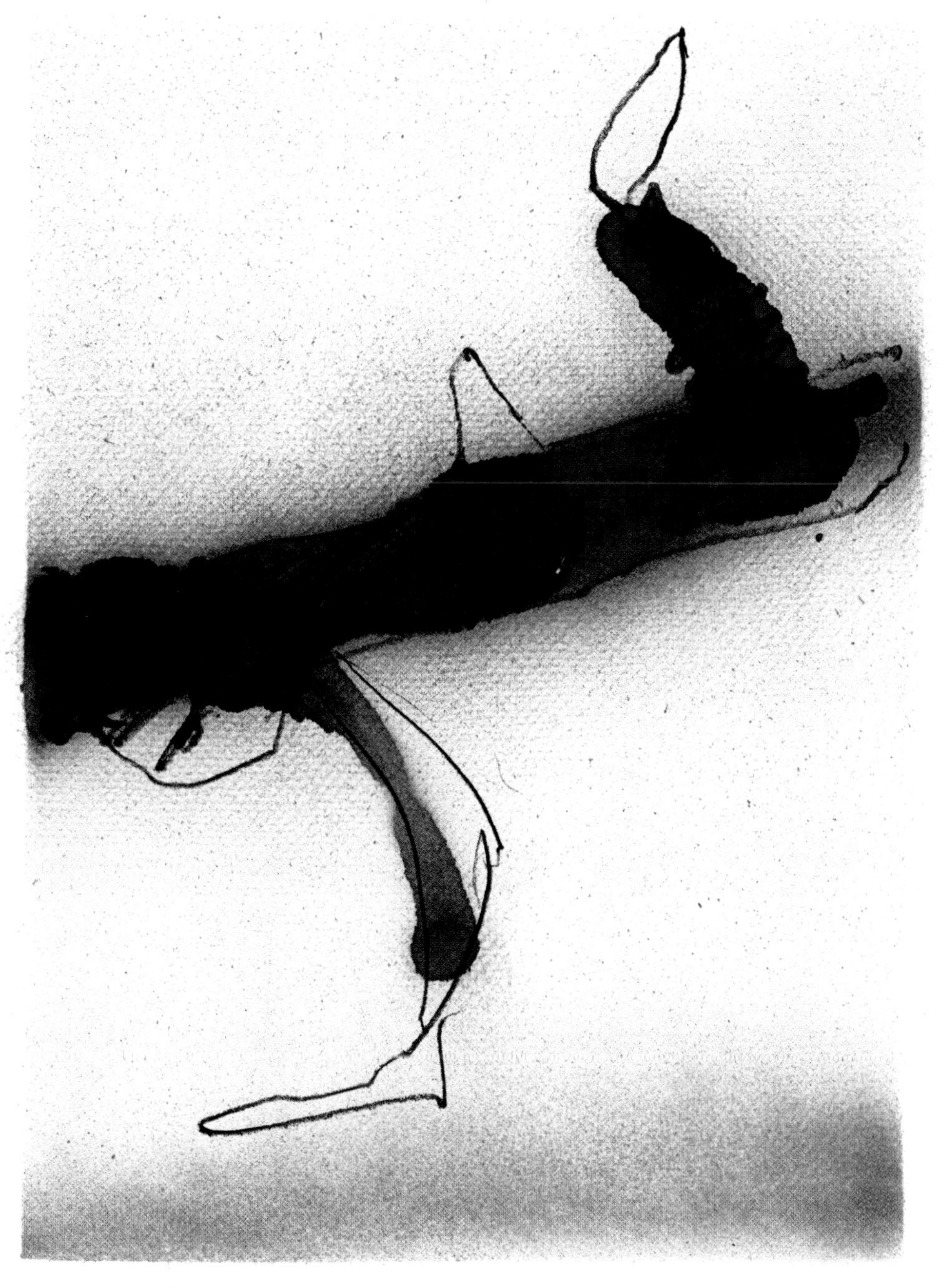

Keep fit and they wont catch you!

She didn't read
but ~~would~~ went to
book shops.

She felt sad,
it seemed to work.

She waved goodbye to her visitors.
The large hand knitted cardigan moved expressively.
She was glad to see the back of them.

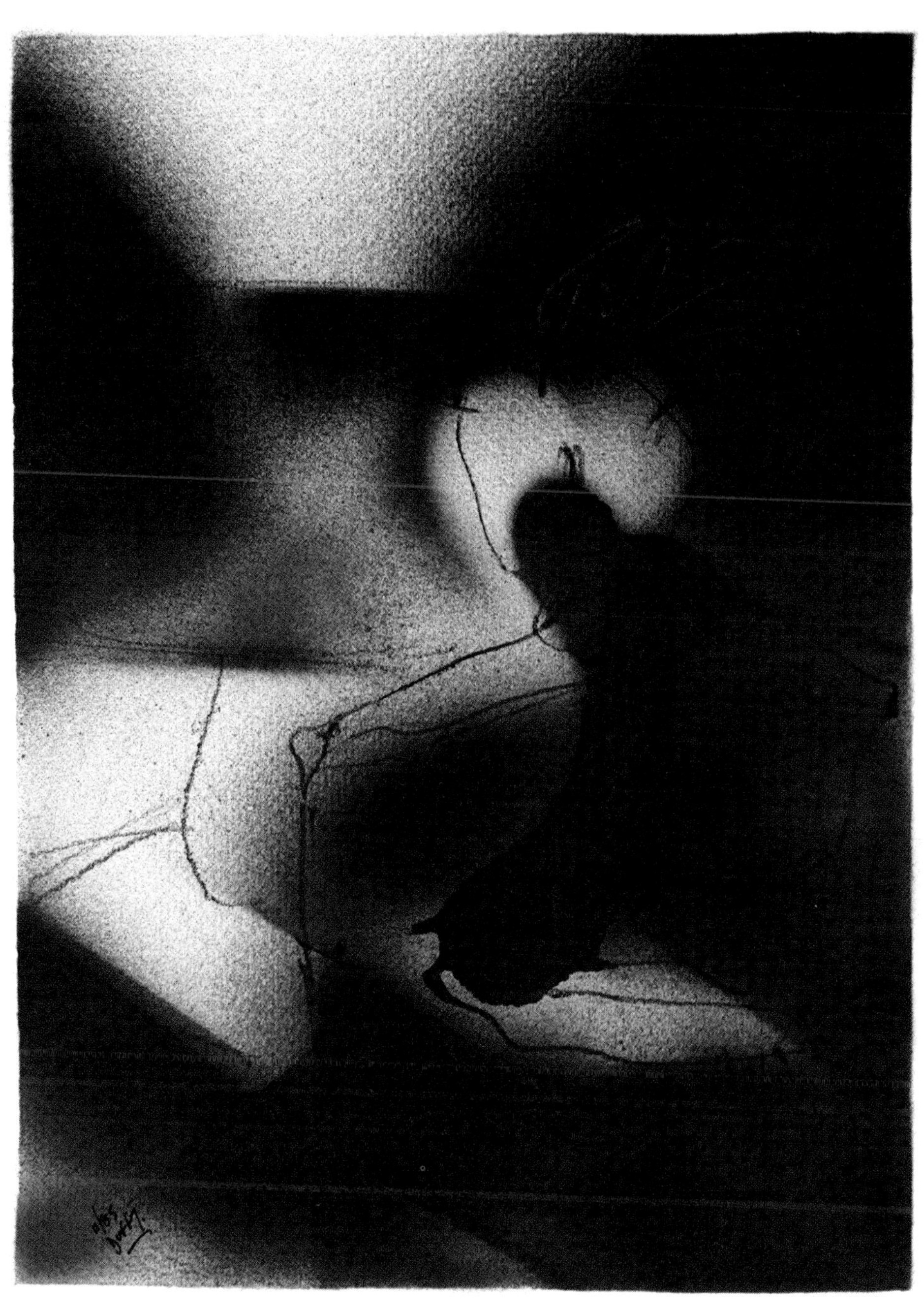

She sat alone
feeling liberated.

Having a 'house husband' was enjoyable.
On the sabbath she would walk around
house projecting her PRESENCE!

She criticised the girls for being coy, She criticised the men for being boys,
But in the her pin stripe demob suit, short back and sides, she would
accept no suppression and pass wind with notable <u>poise</u>.